Explore the World of
Amazing Animals

Text by Mark Carwardine
Illustrated by Jim Channell

W9-BHW-245

A GOLDEN BOOK • NEW YORK

Western Publishing Company, Inc., Racine, Wisconsin 53404

© 1991 Ilex Publishers Limited. Printed in Singapore. All rights reserved. No part of this publication may be reproduced in any form without the prior written permission of the copyright owner. All trademarks are the property of Western Publishing Company, Inc. Library of Congress Catalog Card Number: 91-70175 ISBN: 0-307-15599-4/ISBN: 0-307-65606-3 (lib. bdg.) A MCMXCI

Contents

Why do musk oxen stand in a circle?

Musk oxen have a very clever way of dealing with wolves and other predators. They bunch together in a tight circle or semicircle, and the adults face the attackers with their curved horns pointing outward. Every so often — and completely unexpectedly — one of the adults charges out to gore the enemy.

How does a Japanese macaque keep warm?

Japanese macaques keep warm by taking hot baths regularly. Also called snow monkeys, they live high up in the mountains of Japan. During very bad winters there, the temperature often drops below freezing, and the snow can be more than three feet deep. The macaques get very cold, especially when their long, shaggy coats are soaking wet. But they have learned that the water from volcanic springs in the area is nice and hot. To escape the cold, they sit in these springs with the water up to their necks and their heads out of the water. Unfortunately, in snowstorms, their heads often get covered with snow that may be several inches thick on top.

More about the Japanese macaque

Japanese macaques live in large groups. Normally between one hundred and fifty and two hundred live together.

Japanese macaques spend most of their time bathing or searching for fruit or leaves, or insects or other small animals to eat. Some of them wash their food in fresh water; others dip it in the sea because they like the salty taste.

Japanese macaques learn very quickly and are able to teach one another different tricks. Some even carry food while they walk on two legs like human beings.

Macaques have always played a special role in Japanese myths, stories, and art. They are used to represent the wisdom of Buddha: "See no evil, hear no evil, speak no evil" — one covers his eyes, another his ears, and the third his mouth.

Why does a sea otter tie itself up in seaweed?

Most of a sea otter's life is spent at sea. It only climbs onto land during bad storms. The sea otter even sleeps in the water. But sleeping adrift could be very dangerous because the otter might get carried out to sea by strong ocean currents. Before settling down for a nap, the sea otter wraps kelp around its body. Kelp is a large seaweed attached to the bottom, with large pieces that float close to the surface. Sea otters sleep all night tied up in this giant seaweed. They often gather in small groups for company.

More about the sea otter

Sea otters live along the rocky coasts of the north Pacific Ocean in western North America and eastern Russia.

When they are asleep, sea otters sometimes cover their eyes with their paws.

Baby sea otters are born in the water and ride on their mothers' chests for the first six or seven weeks of their lives. Then they begin taking lessons in swimming, diving, and catching food.

They are excellent swimmers, paddling with their hind legs and using their tails as oars. But sea otters are afraid of drifting too far out to sea and never like to lose sight of land.

Like some monkeys and apes, sea otters are among the few mammals that use tools.

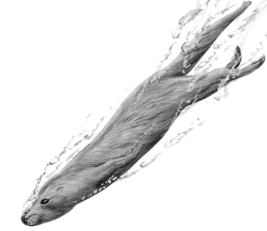

Sea otters can dive to depths of about one hundred and thirty feet to catch crabs, mussels, and other animals. Using their chests as tables, they crack open the shells with a stone and then eat while floating on their backs!

Where does a clown fish live?

Clown fish live among the stinging tentacles of sea anemones on coral reefs. When predators chase them, they dive into the safety of the tentacles and, as a result, usually escape unharmed. A really determined predator that foolishly continues the chase will get stung by the anemone's tentacles and may die. No one knows exactly how the brightly colored clown fish avoid being stung themselves. In return for this protection, the clown fish keep their anemones spotlessly clean by eating all the little pieces of debris that collect on the anemones' tentacles.

More about baby animals

What are the main enemies of a baby zebra?
Lions, hyenas, and wild dogs will all eat baby zebras if they can catch them. Baby zebras are able to walk within an hour of being born, so with enough warning even young zebras can escape from predators.

Why do young bush babies make clicking noises?
At first, a young bush baby is usually "parked" on a branch while its mother searches for food. But when it is a little older, it follows her around. If it cannot keep up, it makes a clicking call which tells her to come back or slow down.

How does a chimpanzee carry her baby?
A female chimpanzee cradles her baby as it clings to the hair on her belly. When it is a little older, she encourages it to ride around on her back, just like a little person riding a horse. Eventually, she lets it walk on its own, but often holds its hand so that it does not get lost.

How strong is a llama?

The South American llama has been trained by people to carry up to 66-pound loads strapped to its back. Young llamas are also very strong. They can walk in less than half an hour after being born.

Where does a baby kangaroo live?

Kangaroos usually have one tiny baby, called a joey, which spends the first few months of its life in a special pouch on its mother's belly. As soon as it is born, the joey crawls into the safety of the pouch and stays there until it is ready to venture out.

Where does the loggerhead turtle lay its eggs?

Loggerhead turtles come ashore to lay their round white eggs in the sand. When their eggs hatch, the baby turtles scurry down to the water's edge, and swim out to sea.

What is so special about a ring-tailed lemur's tail?

Ring-tailed lemurs are easily recognized by their black-and-white tails. These are always held in the air, in the shape of a question mark, when they are walking or running along the ground. Adult lemurs use them like flags, to show their companions exactly where they are. The babies also hold up their tails, even though they spend most of their time riding around on their mothers' backs.

Why do gavials watch their nests?

Gavials lay their eggs in holes in the ground, close to the river. They watch the eggs from a safe distance to make sure that they are not stolen by mongooses, lizards, or people.

13

How does an elephant use its trunk?

An elephant's trunk has many different uses. The animal can use it to pick fruit from high up in a tree, smell and touch things, and throw dust over its back while it is having a dust bath. The trunk is also used for drinking, by sucking up water and squirting it into the elephant's mouth, or as a loudspeaker for amplifying its trumpeting calls. Perhaps the most unusual use, however, is as a snorkel. As an elephant walks underwater along the bottom of a river or lake, it holds its trunk in the air to breathe.

More about the elephant

There are two kinds of elephant: One lives on the plains and in the woodlands of Africa, the other mainly in the forests of Asia. African elephants are the bigger of the two, with larger ears and tusks.

Elephants are *herbivores* — animals that do not eat meat. They eat grass, leaves, fruit, and the bark of trees. If the uppermost leaves are out of reach, elephants simply push the whole tree over!

An elephant may live as long as sixty years. The elephant's tusks are special teeth that grow throughout its life. They are the largest teeth of any animal. Unfortunately, they are very valuable for carving ornaments and other items. Hundreds of thousands of elephants have been killed in Africa by people who sell the tusks to make money.

Elephants are intelligent animals and very strong. In Asia, people train them to work lifting and carrying logs. They also appear in ceremonial processions in India, wearing golden decorations.

A baby elephant is nearly three feet tall when it is born. Sometimes it sucks its trunk, just as a human baby sucks its thumb!

How far does an arctic tern fly in its lifetime?

The arctic tern is one of the greatest travelers in the animal kingdom. Every year, some individuals fly from one end of the world to the other — between the Arctic and the Antarctic — and back again. They breed in the north during the Arctic summer, then fly south for the Antarctic summer. This requires a round-trip journey of nearly twenty-five thousand miles and involves flying nonstop for no less than eight months of the year. In its lifetime of about twenty-five years, an arctic tern flies far enough to travel to the moon and back.

More about the arctic tern

Arctic terns live near the sea, where they feed on fish, squid, and other small animals. Flying low over the water, they carefully search for their food. They hover a few feet above the surface and then dive in headfirst for the catch.

Anyone entering an arctic tern colony is likely to get dive-bombed by the angry birds. They sometimes strike hard with their daggerlike bills — while fiercely defending their eggs and chicks from people and other predators.

Arctic terns have been recorded nesting within a hundred miles or so of the North Pole. They usually mate for life, the same females and males always breeding together.

What does a narwhal do with its sword?

No one knows for certain what the narwhal's sword, or tusk, is for, but there are many different theories. It might be used to break through ice on the surface of the sea in the cold waters of the animal's Arctic home. It could be used to skewer fish and other prey or to search the bottom for food. Most likely, however, it is a kind of weapon. Narwhals have been seen using them like swords, fencing together on the ocean surface. This may be quite common, for many of the animals, particularly males, have nasty scars, and broken tusks. One was even spotted with another's broken tusk sticking out of its head.

More about animals and their food

How do pelicans use their beaks?
Pelicans use the enormous pouches on their beaks as nets to catch fish underwater. Sometimes they dive from the air above, but usually they sit on the surface, working together in "fishing schools." All the birds in a school surround and trap shoals of fish, then submerge their heads and necks to scoop them up.

Where does a snowy owl find its food?
Snowy owls are large and powerful birds. Lemmings are their favorite food but they also hunt arctic hares, ground squirrels, and many other animals living on the freezing cold Arctic tundra where they live.

What does a slow loris eat?
Slow lorises eat snails, insects, lizards, birds, other small animals and fruit. They never seem to be in a hurry and move almost in slow motion. But they can strike their prey with incredible speed and give a quick, painful bite.

Why does a duckbilled platypus have a "beak"?
The duckbilled platypus uses its sensitive beak, or snout, to find food, because, when diving, it closes its eyes and ears and cannot see or hear a thing. It simply feels around for underwater creatures.

Why don't mouse lemurs feed all year round?

Mouse lemurs feed alone at night on a variety of small animals such as beetles, spiders, and frogs. During the dry season they rest, and hibernate in hollow trees. In their deep sleep, they go completely still and eat virtually nothing.

How do screech owls catch moths?

Most screech owls are fairly small birds (some are no bigger than a robin), and they feed mainly on moths and other insects. They can catch a moth in midair, with a loud snap of their bills, or seize it on the ground, or on a branch, with their feet.

What is a manatee?

A manatee is a little like a water-dwelling cow. In fact, it is often known as the "sea cow" or "fish cow" because it grazes on water grasses and other plants. When looking for food, it sometimes "walks" along the bottom on its flippers.

Where does a moose find its favorite food?

Moose are fond of ponds and marshes. Water plants are among their favorite foods, and the animals sometimes disappear under the water's surface in their eagerness to find them.

Where does a cuckoo lay its eggs?

A female cuckoo lays her eggs in the nests of other birds. She is very secretive and waits until the owners are out of sight before approaching. A single egg is laid in each nest. The cuckoo then removes one of the eggs already in the nest to keep the number the same. She continues doing this every other day until she has laid a total of eight to twelve eggs. Meanwhile, the unfortunate nest owners begin incubating, completely unaware of what has happened. The baby cuckoos usually hatch first and, almost immediately, they push all the other eggs — or young, if there are any — out of the nests.

More about the cuckoo

Of the 127 different species of cuckoos, only about one third of them lay their eggs in other birds' nests.

Female cuckoos usually choose host birds much smaller than themselves. But following generations always choose the same host. Cuckoos that live in the United States do not use other birds' nests at all, but some cowbirds do.

A cuckoo egg *(above left)* usually looks very similar to the other eggs in the nest.

Only the male European cuckoo makes the familiar "cuckoo-cuckoo" call. The female makes a gurgling or chuckling call.

Why does a praying mantis pray?

A praying mantis will spend hours sitting in a tree or bush with its forelegs held together as if in prayer. It is not really praying, of course. It is lying in wait for passing insects. Beautifully camouflaged, with a body and legs shaped and colored like a leaf, flower, or twig, the praying mantis looks so much like a part of the plant on which it waits that it is almost invisible. The mantis either remains completely motionless or gently sways from side to side as if in a breeze. As soon as an insect comes within range — unaware of the hidden danger — the mantis's forelegs suddenly shoot forward and grab the unfortunate creature. Held in a pincerlike grip, the insect cannot escape. It becomes a meal for the praying mantis.

More about the praying mantis

There are more than eighteen hundred different species of praying mantis, and some are as much as six inches long.

Most praying mantises eat insects such as flies, grasshoppers, and caterpillars, but they occasionally take spiders and other small animals. Sometimes they eat other mantises.

Being a male mantis can be dangerous because there is a very good chance of being eaten by a female. She nearly always eats the head first, while holding him in a pincerlike grip.

Praying mantises are so well camouflaged that they are not seen by most of the predators that hunt them. If they are attacked, they strike out with their strong front legs, which have sharp spines and can inflict painful jabs.

How long can a Weddell seal hold its breath underwater?

A Weddell seal can hold its breath for up to an hour. It dives deeper — and longer — than any other seal, regularly going down to more than nine hundred feet below the surface of the sea. One was recorded in a dive to about two thousand feet, and it remained submerged for seventy-three minutes! Young Weddell seals begin to dive when they are only a week old. For the first two months of their lives they practice diving and swimming every day. At first they cannot hold their breath for as long as their parents.

More about the Weddell seal

The freezing-cold waters of the Antarctic are home to Weddell seals. In these areas the sea is often frozen to a depth of several feet for eight months of the year. The protruding front, or "buck," teeth are used to gnaw through the sea ice when the seals need to breathe.

Weddell seals have very large eyes that help them see in the murky depths.

In the Antarctic winter, Weddell seals spend most of their time in the water. They can sometimes be heard calling to one another.

Weddell seals feed on fish, squid, octopus, shrimp, and other animals. One seal was seen catching a fish that was nearly five feet long. It took the seal three hours to eat this big catch.

Unlike many seals, the Weddell has no fear of people. Instead of trying to escape, it often rolls onto its side and holds a flipper in the air.

More about dangerous animals

What do lions eat?
Lions live on the hot, dry, grassy plains of Africa.
They eat many different kinds of animals, including
wildebeest, zebras, and warthogs. The females do
most of the hunting. The males' furry manes make
them too easy to see, so their chief role is to
defend their prides or families from enemies and
other intruders.

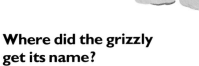

**Where did the grizzly
get its name?**
Grizzlies are called that
because their coats look
grizzled (or streaked with
gray) not because they are
bad-tempered. However,
they can be very dangerous
and fight using "bear hugs."

Where do hippos go at night?
The hippo is one of Africa's biggest and most
dangerous animals. Hippos spend most of the
daytime sleeping and resting in lakes and rivers.
But they are very active at night, when they leave
the water and walk long distances to their favorite
grazing areas, which are known as "hippo lawns."

What are crocodiles mistaken for?
Crocodiles are well camouflaged. They wait
quietly along the edge of rivers and lakes, ready to
attack unsuspecting animals, such as deer and
monkeys, when they come down to the water's
edge to drink. They make so little noise — and lie
so still — that they are often mistaken for logs.

How dangerous is a puff adder?

Most snakes are completely harmless creatures. But there is no doubt that some of them are very dangerous. One of these is the puff adder, which is the commonest poisonous snake in Africa. It can lunge forward and bite so quickly that it is difficult to escape.

How dangerous is a vampire bat?

Although many people are afraid of bats, they are generally harmless creatures. The vampire bat is the only one which is at all dangerous — and it rarely attacks people. It lives in Central and South America, where it feeds on the blood of other animals.

Why don't all sharks attack people?

The shark is probably the most feared animal in the world. With its streamlined body, needle-sharp teeth, glaring eyes, and a nose that can smell food from miles away, it has a terrible reputation. But not all sharks are dangerous. Most of them eat mainly fish and are quite frightened of people.

Why does a mandrill act like a spoiled child?

Mandrills often act like spoiled children when they are cross. These large monkeys grunt, chatter and shake their heads. When they get really angry they can be vicious and sometimes kill other animals.

29

What does a blue whale eat?

The blue whale is the largest animal that has ever lived on earth. Despite its enormous size, the blue whale feeds entirely on shrimplike creatures called krill. Some krill are less than one inch long. The whale must eat literally millions of them every day to survive. It swims into a dense school of krill and captures as many as it can with a single gulp of its enormous mouth. The water is filtered out through special strainers, leaving all the krill trapped inside. On a good day, an adult blue whale may swallow up to four tons of krill. This is equivalent to about four million of the tiny animals.

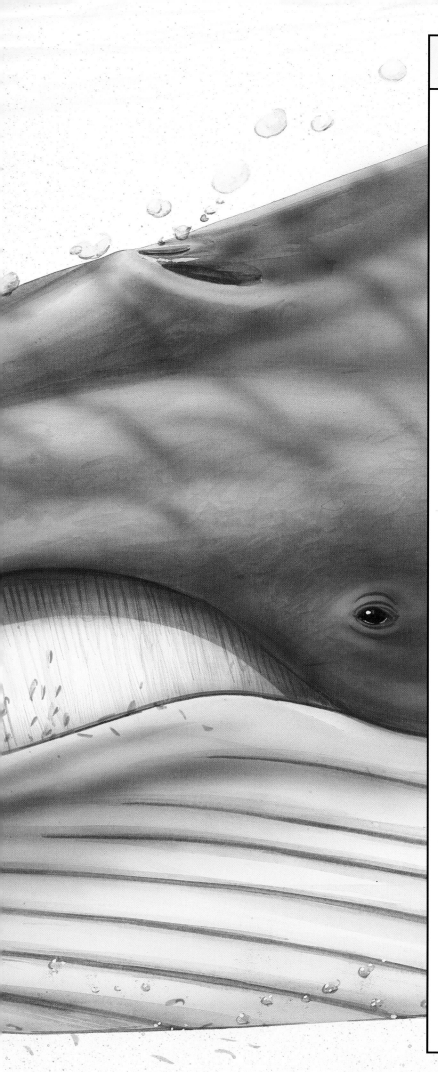

More about the blue whale

An adult blue whale weighs up to one hundred and fifty tons and may be one hundred feet long. It is bigger than the largest of all the dinosaurs. Even baby blue whales are about twenty feet long and weigh as much as eight tons when they are born.

Blue whales are mammals (not fish), so they have to come to the surface to breathe. Before taking in a new supply of air, they exhale through their blowhole, spouting water into the air.

Feeding takes place only during the summer months. For the rest of the year, blue whales probably do not eat at all.

Blue whales are found in all the oceans of the world, but so many have been killed by whalers they are now very rare.

Where do salmon lay their eggs?

Every year enormous numbers of salmon set off on an extraordinary and dangerous migration. They swim great distances from the sea to the upper stretches of rivers to spawn. Battling powerful currents and leaping waterfalls as high as fifteen feet, they return to the very same spot in the river where they themselves hatched years before. When they arrive, the female salmon lay their eggs in shallow depressions in the riverbed and the males fertilize them. Pacific salmon are too exhausted after their spawning run to journey back to the sea. Some Atlantic salmon make three or four spawning runs during their lifetime.

More about the salmon

Salmon eggs hatch in about three months, but usually the young fish do not migrate to the sea until they are three or four years old.

According to their age and size, salmon are given different names. Newly hatched salmon are called *fry*. When they are a few inches long, they are known as *parr*. As soon as they are old enough to migrate to the sea, they are called *smolt*. Adults are called *salmon*, but once they have bred, they are known as *kelt*.

While they are migrating up the rivers, the salmon do not feed. By the time they reach the spawning area, many of them have lost as much as half their original body weight.

33

How does a giant snake kill its prey?

Many stories about such giant snakes as boa constrictors, pythons, and anacondas are inaccurate and exaggerations. Despite popular belief, they do not constrict suddenly or crush their victims to death by breaking every bone in their bodies. The truth is less dramatic but no less gruesome. The snake first catches its prey with a painful bite, which is not poisonous. It gets a firm grip by using its curved teeth and powerful jaws. Then it coils its long body around the unfortunate animal and waits. Each time its victim breathes out, the snake squeezes a little tighter. The animal eventually dies, sometimes after several hours, simply because it can no longer breathe.

More about giant snakes

The anaconda is the heaviest snake in the world. Stories of it reaching one hundred and thirty feet or more in length are completely untrue, however. The longest ever recorded was about thirty-three feet.

Large constricting snakes probably could kill a person and without too much trouble. Fortunately, they prefer to eat birds, turtles, caimans, and other wild animals.

Unlike many snakes that lay eggs, boa constrictors and anacondas give birth to live young.

Anacondas live in tropical South America. They often bask in the sun on branches overhanging large rivers, swamps, and lakes.

35

Why does a howler monkey howl?

Every morning just as the sun begins to rise, loud howls and cries come from the treetops in the Amazon jungle. This strange dawn chorus can be heard for more than three miles. The calls, which are among the loudest of any animal's in the world, are made by howler monkeys. They call as loudly as they can at dawn every morning — and again at intervals during the day — to keep other howler monkeys away from their favorite trees. By listening to the various howls from neighboring troops, all the monkeys in the area can avoid meeting one another — and fighting — as they travel through the trees in search of food.

Howler monkeys eat mostly leaves and fruit. Often they hang upside down from branches, using only their long and flexible tails. This leaves their hands and feet free for feeding.

More about rare animals

How rare is the golden lion tamarin?

A spectacular golden color all over, golden lion tamarins look just like small lions. Of all the monkeys and apes, they are among the rarest, because people burn down their jungle homes and even capture the animals to sell as pets and to zoos. There are just over a hundred golden lion tamarins surviving in the wild, in only two areas of jungle in Brazil.

Where can you see a mountain gorilla?

There are three different kinds of gorilla and the mountain gorilla is the rarest. Fewer than four hundred of them are left in the wild and they all live in a beautiful mountainous area of central Africa called the Virunga Volcanoes.

Why is the giant panda so famous?

The giant panda is one of the rarest animals in the world. There are fewer than a thousand survivors living in the remote bamboo forests of southwestern China. The panda is well known for its beautiful thick black-and-white coat. But it is most famous as the symbol of the World Wildlife Fund.

What games do polar bears play?

Polar bears love to have pretend fights and enjoy tobogganing (they slide down snowbanks on their bellies). There are only about twenty-five thousand polar bears in the wild.

Where does the Amazon river dolphin live?

As its name suggests, the Amazon river dolphin lives in the rivers and creeks of the Amazon jungle. It is threatened by hunting, dams, and pollution.

Why has the Tasmanian tiger been declared extinct?

Tasmanian tigers were once common animals on the Australian island of Tasmania. But so many have been killed by hunters and by disease that there are probably none left. The last known member of the species died in a zoo in 1936. Since then, there have been many expeditions to look for survivors, just in case there are any left, but none have been found — so the animal has officially been declared extinct.

What is an aye-aye?

The aye-aye looks like a strange creature from outer space. It has ratlike teeth, a bushy, squirrellike tail, a catlike body, and huge eyes and ears. Closely related to a group of primates known as the lemurs, it is extremely rare and only found on the island of Madagascar.

How does the Malayan tapir keep cool?

Malayan tapirs live in the steamy jungles of Southeast Asia. They are excellent swimmers and often lounge around in water during the hottest part of the day. They are very rare animals and, despite their bold markings, surprisingly difficult to see.

What is a leafy sea dragon?

One of the strangest creatures of the sea, the leafy sea dragon is a kind of sea horse that lives among seaweed around the coasts of Australia. It looks as though it is covered with pieces of seaweed, but these growths are actually parts of its body. The sea dragon's disguise as a piece of floating seaweed is one of the most bizarre examples of camouflage in nature. The camouflage makes the leafy sea dragon almost invisible to both its predators and to its prey. It floats confidently among the seaweed, sucking up its favorite food — tiny prawnlike creatures — with its long, narrow snout, knowing that it will not be seen.

More about the leafy sea dragon

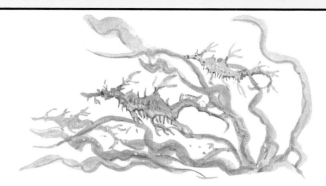

When leafy sea dragons are born, they are only slightly more than an inch long, but already their weedy disguise is well formed. When they are fully grown they measure about twelve inches long.

Despite their unusual shape, sea horses are fish. They are very weak swimmers, however, and the only way they avoid being carried along by even the slightest ocean currents is by clinging to the nearest seaweed with their grasping tails.

The female sea horse lays her eggs inside a pouch underneath the male's tail. When they hatch, the baby sea horses stay inside this pouch and are carried around by their father.

A sea horse uses the fin on its back as a kind of propeller. With this fluttering fin, it moves elegantly through the coral reefs and seaweed forests where it lives.

Where does a butterfly go in the winter?

In many parts of the world, the long winter months are a difficult time for butterflies. They usually hibernate. Some butterflies such as tortoiseshells, peacocks, and a few others hibernate as adults. They settle in a dry, sheltered spot in the autumn and stay there until the warmer weather returns in the spring. During warm spells, they may wake up and fly around, but for the most part, they do not move for months. Many butterflies live very short lives. They die toward the end of summer or in autumn, often when they are only a few weeks old. The species survive the winter as eggs or caterpillars, or in cocoons.

More about butterflies

Butterflies generally fly by day; moths at night. Butterflies hold their wings closed and over their backs when at rest; moths usually fold their wings flat. Butterflies typically have clublike antennae; moths have feathery antennae.

There are more than one hundred and fifty thousand different kinds of moth in the world and only about fifteen thousand kinds of butterfly.

Butterflies have to warm themselves up before they can fly. They usually do this by sitting in the sun, which is one of the reasons why few butterflies are seen flying on cloudy days.

Certain butterflies migrate long distances. The record holder is the monarch butterfly, which winters in California and Mexico, then flies as far as eighteen hundred miles north to breed.

How does a bat "see" in the dark?

Most bats are active only at night, yet they have poor eyesight and cannot see where they are going. To find their way in the dark, they rely on a system called echolocation that enables them to build up a "sound picture" of everything around them. The bats make a series of short, sharp calls. These are often very loud, but they are pitched too high for us to hear. The bats pick up the echoes of the sounds when they bounce back from trees, buildings, insects, or other objects in their path. The bats can tell if an object is moving, how far away it is, its size, and what it is made of.

More about bats

More than 950 species of bat are found in different habitats all around the world except in the Arctic, the Antarctic, and on the highest mountains.

Bats range in size from the tiny bumblebee bat, with a wingspan of only about six inches, to the giant flying foxes, with wingspans as great as six and a half feet.

The different kinds of bat feed on different foods, ranging from insects, frogs, lizards, and even fish to pollen and nectar.

Not all bats have poor eyesight. Many fruit bats have very large eyes and navigate by sight rather than echolocation.

Some moths can hear the calls bats make when they are hunting and have learned to keep away.

INDEX

AN ILEX BOOK
Created and produced by Ilex Publishers Limited
29-31 George Street, Oxford, OX1 2AJ

Main illustrations by Jim Channell/Bernard Thornton Artists
Other illustrations by Jim Channell and Martin Camm/Bernard Thornton Artists